P9-DWJ-430

PRAYERS FOR PAGANS AND HYPOCRITES

Also by Peter De Rosa

BLESS ME, FATHER

(under the name of Neil Boyd)

CLYDE EDMISTON

PRAYERS FOR PAGANS AND HYPOCRITES

by Peter De Rosa

ILLUSTRATIONS BY HARO

WILLIAM MORROW AND COMPANY, INC.
NEW YORK 1979

Originally published in Great Britain in 1977 by William Collins Sons & Co., Ltd.

Library of Congress Cataloging in Publication Data

De Rosa, Peter.
Prayers for pagans and hypocrites.

1. Christian life–Anecdote, facetiae, satire, etc.
I. Title
BV4501.2.D48 1979 248 78-27802
ISBN 0-688-03349-7

BOOK DESIGN CARL WEISS

Printed in the United States of America.

First U.S. Edition

1 2 3 4 5 6 7 8 9 10

In Gratitude

to

Mary, Francis and Daniel

for Not Providing Me

with Any of the Material

for This Book

INTRODUCTION

RELIGION HAS A QUITE UNJUSTIFIED REPUTATION FOR BEING humourless and melancholy. The deadpan expression on the faces of clergy and congregation during services masks their tremendous hilarity of soul and prevents the unbeliever from perceiving that churches have completely ousted the music halls of old as the bastions of mirth.

Many a time have I walked into a church and witnessed the whole assembly reciting together–without so much as the twitch of an eyebrow–the most astonishingly amusing prayers, one after another. I could only marvel at the self-discipline which held them back from rolling in the aisles. For I swear I heard them in solemn Sunday rows pleading with God for what they desperately didn't want, confessing a hearty sorrow for sin they did not in the least feel and praising the Almighty when they passionately wanted to wring His sacred neck. Funniest of all, I suppose, were the bland appeals–loudest and clearest from the bourgeoisie–to be rendered poor and crucified. I was obliged to hasten out of the building on all fours before I disgraced myself.

It must be of some significance that when worshippers are asked to recite the most amusing prayer they know, they invariably select St. Augustine's "Lord, give me chastity, but not yet." Even as they utter it, they dissolve in uncharacteristic mirth. Now, in my view, there is something approaching genius in such dissimulation. How could the uninitiated surmise that their merriment is but a smoke screen behind which the godly hide the real black comedy of faith?

Pause for a moment to ask yourself, how is it possible for a normal person to find anything remotely funny in Augustine's prayer? It is positively dull, prosaic, commonplace. Has there ever been a pious, pimply youth who did not voice it spontaneously in the heat of the moment? I distinctly recall that when I was in my teens I used to resort to it three times a day before breakfast and times without number after supper.

Augustine would, I grant, have merited the laughter of his co-religionists had he prayed, "Lord, give me chastity *right now.*" What a sublime mixture of humour and pathos there is in that improbable line. In its essence, it is as funny as a brothel keeper imploring God to improve the moral character of the neighbourhood or my son going down on his knees and pleading, "No pocket-money for me this week, Daddy, I don't deserve it."

It is hardly necessary to remark that almost without exception prayers offered in religious establishments follow this farcical pattern. The overall effect is such that the combined wit of Voltaire, Swift and Bernard Shaw could hardly have improved on it. "Grant that we may be always truly wise." "Forgive us as we forgive." "Thy will be done on Earth as it is in Heaven." As if those who mouth such imprecations did not know that, were God to answer them, it would lead to an impossible state of affairs.

In vivid contrast, the prayers in this book are all–like Augustine's honest appeal for a postponed and less inconvenient chastity–deadly dull. This is because they reflect exactly how we pray in those numinous moments when we are not aware of saying our prayers.

I do not deny that the human heart is capable of aspirations far higher than any I record. I simply maintain that they occur with stunning irregularity. Anyone who feels such aspirations coming on can easily gratify them by taking part in any Sunday service or picking up a well-thumbed manual of prayers. Indeed, he won't have to *alter* any of his usual devotions, only *mean* them.

I realize that, for all my pains, I run the risk of being labelled a killjoy. Many worshippers, exhibiting the fruits of their devotions, will never forgive me for proving that parsons are comedians in disguise. They will even accuse me of being an apostate or an infidel for exposing so relentlessly the ruses of religion.

What can I say in my defense except that, in my view, it is time to call a halt to traditional religious frivolity. I am keen to reroute "devout" people from a mock to a genuine seriousness. Life is far too bruising a business for humans to go on praying as though they were angelic beings or saints already pensioned off in Paradise. Hence I am proposing in this book a more honest if platitudinous type of prayer more in keeping with man's fundamental lack of rectitude.

In a word, my aim is to encourage you, my prospective readers, to pray as God wants and expects you to pray: like the pagans and hypocrites you are.

PRAYERS
FOR
PAGANS
AND
HYPOCRITES

1

LOVING THE GHASTLY NEIGHBOUR

Has it never occurred to You, Lord, that some neighbours don't want to be loved?

□ □

All right, God, I promise to love my neighbour, provided that doesn't include the people next door.

□ □

As soon as I went out of my way to be helpful to G. G. Winklemann he suspected me of having an affair with his wife.

The last time I offered my neighbour the hand of friend-ship he threw me straight over his shoulder.

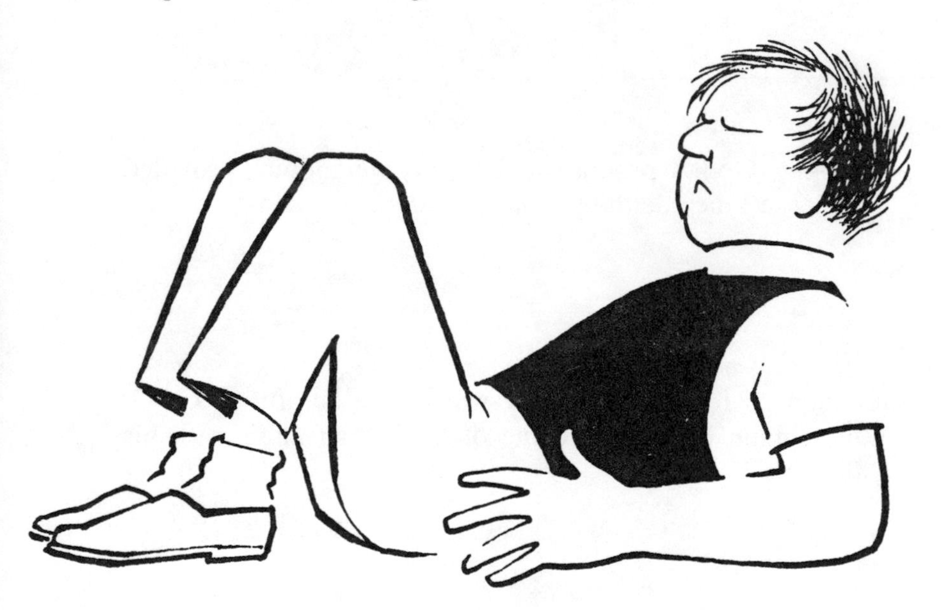

I find it relatively easy loving my enemies. It's my friends I can't stand.

The sad thing is, Lord, that in my experience, it's the worst enemies who make the best neighbours.

□ □

After all my efforts to give him a bit of good neighbourly advice, that fat slob Connors turned on me and said, "And to think that once you were my friend."

□ □

I'm getting an awful lot of fun out of trying to love others. I haven't seen *that* look on people's faces since I started to learn to drive.

Now what do we do? Our neighbours have just got up this monster petition imploring us to quit the neighbourhood.

Love is patient, courteous, kind and utterly impossible.

In my opinion, Lord, if You cracked down on Your enemies instead of loving them You'd soon have lots more friends.

□ □

When I tried to be kind to the thug I work with, he said, "Who are you trying to punish, yourself or me?"

□ □

Practicing charity certainly has its complications. Outside the church this morning I invited Harry Stoat to dinner because I don't like him, and because he doesn't like me he accepted.

□ □

Might it be, Lord, that love is a solution that is infinitely worse than the problem?

2

BLINDING PEOPLE WITH SILENCE

O my God, I realize nobody ever listens to Willy, but if You've ever heard him You'll know why.

But if I give Gary my undivided attention he may be deluded into thinking that he's interesting.

□ □

To be honest, Lord, I wasn't actually listening to James. I just found him far too boring to talk to.

□ □

I never can make up my mind whether You're listening to me or You've left the room.

Over the years, my wife and I have become such
good listeners that we don't talk to each other any more.

When Jack's wife walked out on him, I listened to him for four solid hours, and afterwards he complained that he hadn't got *anything* out of our conversation.

□ □

Dean and Debbie like arguing, Lord, because the only things they have in common are their disagreements.

I have listened very carefully to the Reverend Perkins' point of view, and now I despise him more than ever.

I confess I made sure that the scandal spread around the parish by putting Pete under oath not to tell anybody but his wife.

Ever since I closed my ears to gossip, Lord, I have this weird feeling that everyone's talking about *me.*

□ □

Dobson is a man of such utter integrity, I feel I can't trust him.

Lord, I wouldn't mind listening to old Mrs. Crusky describing all her aches and pains if only it didn't give her so much pleasure.

□ □

I took Your advice, Lord, and kept silent in face of Theo's vile accusations and now he's going round telling everyone I didn't deny it.

□ □

I leave the choice to You. Shall I break my silence or his neck?

3

THE WAGGER

When I stopped arguing with Margaret and listened to her for the first time with any interest, she paused for a moment and said, "You really despise me, don't you?"

Imagine making people with fast tongues and no brakes.

□ □

I was having this long, exhilarating, illuminating conversation with Ken Bostock, Lord, when he ruined it by joining in.

□ □

My boss says he prefers men who always speak their mind so he doesn't make the mistake of employing them.

I confess, Lord, that I have sinned grievously.
I told my boss that he was the inspiration of us all, which is a lie. I then thanked him warmly for his kindness, discrimination, tact, generosity, and powers of leadership–lies, all of it lies!
So, now I come humbly before You to beg Your pardon and to promise not to tell such lies again until my next chance of promotion.

She obviously likes little arguments, because it keeps her tongue in trim for big arguments.

When that maniac ran into the back of my car I had to swear at him, Lord, or else he would have claimed it was my fault.

□ □

As soon as I said it, I tried to take it back but my wife had cleverly swallowed it.

□ □

I tried to get behind Tony's words, but there were far too many of them.

I enjoy talking to Sarah, Lord, because we like laughing at the same people.

Lies don't bother me, but I won't have those horrible people spreading the truth about me.

Now that I've started thinking *before* I speak, my insults are stupendous.

□ □

You know how it is, Lord. If I didn't say idiotic things sometimes, I'd go crazy.

□ □

Even when my friends let me down and words fail me, I'm not a moaner. I'm a screamer.

□ □

I won't have to account at the Judgment for any idle words. Mine are always very hardworking.

4

FILTHY LUCRE

Granted, money doesn't bring happiness, but it does make misery distinctly endurable.

The effects of affluence on me might be dreadful, but You should see the effects of poverty on my wife and children.

I'm not disputing the fact that the best things in life are free, but you have to be pretty well off to enjoy them.

□ □

Make me fabulously rich, God, and I promise to answer lots of poor people's prayers for You.

□ □

I was hoping it had dawned on You by this time that the only way to take my mind off money is to give me a plentiful supply of the stuff.

□ □

Lord, the great advantage which the frightful problems of wealth have over the frightful problems of poverty is that you can pay people to solve them.

It seems to me that the poor don't object to charity, provided it's given without love.

When I was in my teens, I prayed hard that one day I'd marry a handsome millionaire, have beautiful children and live in a villa in the South of France—and You say *You're* disappointed in *me?*

Level with me, Lord. Could wealth possibly make me a worse Christian than I am now?

□ □

Happy are the poor, You say? No, I can't honestly say I'd ever noticed.

□ □

After Jesus' frightening warning about the rich, I'd start by putting aside a large slice of my wealth for scientific research into the best way to miniaturize camels.

□ □

Thank You very much for telling me that one day You're going to give me a hundredfold, but couldn't I have onefold in advance?

I didn't just marry George for his money, Lord, I also fell madly in love with his possessions.

I'd gladly give my last penny to the poor, but I'm not down to that yet.

□ □

My requests for financial assistance may be mean but at least You can be sure they are sincere.

□ □

I thank You, Father, for the abundance of blue skies and birdsong and lush green grass, for the onset of burgeoning spring and leafy summer, for the swish of the sea and the wind in the tall pines and a frugal meal from time to time.

5

BROUGHT TO MY KNEES

Lord, I clearly prayed,
"Lead me not into temptation,"
so, did You lose Your way?

Yes, it's me. How did You know I was desperate?

□ □

Dear Lord, I beg You not to take my prayers more seriously than they are intended.

□ □

I know what I ought to do, Lord, that's not my problem.

□ □

Why is it that as soon as I settle down to a few precious moments of quiet prayer, You keep on interrupting me?

I know You always answer my prayers, but couldn't You sometimes say Yes?

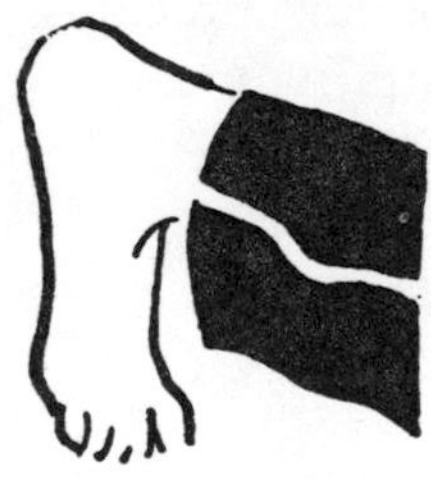

I've reached the stage now where I'm afraid to pray for the sun to rise in the mornings in case it doesn't.

□ □

I firmly believe You exist, O God, because it's simply not possible to put all my unanswered prayers down to chance.

□ □

I suppose I'm inclined to look at it like this, Lord. Prayer makes me feel *I'm* doing something to help even if *You're* not.

Lord, don't You think you should try and overcome
Your distractions during my prayers?

Now, as You suggested, I've knelt down, joined my hands, and closed my eyes–and I swear that if You let any of my kids come through that door, I'll never pray to You again.

□ □

This morning when I awoke my flu had gone, the sun was gleaming in the azure sky, my wife kissed me, my kids had remembered it was my birthday and there was an unexpected check in the mail. There's no need for me to tell You, Father, that I'm warming to You all the time.

□ □

Heavens, You mean the prayer books have got it all wrong and You *don't* like flattery?

□ □

In Your omniscience You know in advance what I'm going to say to You. And because I'm a sinner I know what You are going to have to say to me. So why don't we call a truce and both keep quiet?

Father, not Thy will but mine be done.

The guy next door is praying for a downpour on his garden and I'm praying just as hard for unblemished sunshine for my round of golf, so this is the crunch.

□ □

But You must have known that when I prayed for my colleague to be promoted instead of me I was banking on Your usual response.

□ □

Have a good day, Lord, and I'll see You again tonight, last thing.

6

FAMILY AND FIENDS

Lord, if You hadn't said that all marriages are made in Heaven, I would have sworn that most of them were made in Hong Kong.

It's nice of You to console me with the long-term view, but couldn't You get my family to show me some appreciation before I die?

□ □

We are a family of altruists, God. We're always talking about other people.

□ □

After twenty years of marriage, I too can testify that the family is the basic cell of society.

I don't care how my wife reacts to my infidelities, Lord, provided she doesn't forgive me.

In some ways my wife reminds me of You. She's always complaining that nobody loves her.

□ □

Lord, my wife has been threatening to run out on me so many times I'm beginning to fear she never will.

God, how great You are. At three o'clock this morning when our baby screamed, I stood at the end of his little cot marvelling that such a fragile frame could generate so much power with only one moving part.

□ □

It may be his fifth birthday, Lord, but this time I refuse to forgive the sheer diabolical wickedness of my son and former heir.

Yes, I admit that we prayed for children, but that was before we had any.

If we all have to become as little children to enter the Kingdom of Heaven, all I can say, Lord, is that Heaven must be a hell of a place.

□ □

When I look at the splendid altruistic young people of today, I'm very grateful You let me lose my youthful idealism at a very early age.

7

IT'S ALWAYS TEE-TIME

The ball went in, then out, then in and out, and finally in again. That's when I *knew* You loved me, Lord.

Fore! Oh, please God, I hope he's insured. But why should he be, sitting quietly in a deck chair in his own backyard. Fore! Fore!

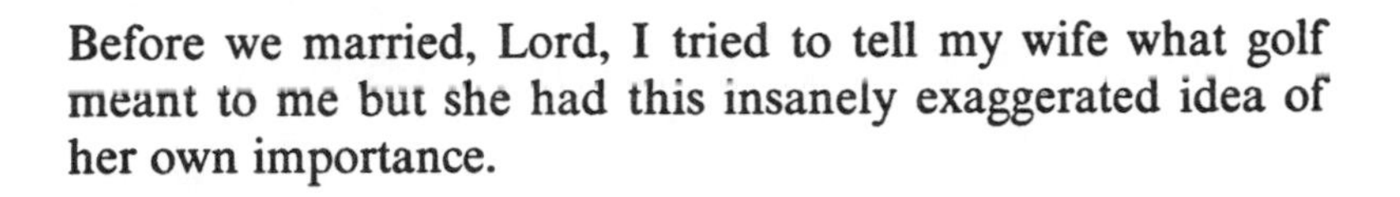

Before we married, Lord, I tried to tell my wife what golf meant to me but she had this insanely exaggerated idea of her own importance.

□ □

Honestly, I *am* thinking of my wife. If I took her to the beach today instead of playing golf I'd only make her miserable.

□ □

It's desperately hard on me, Lord, my only daughter thoughtlessly fixing her wedding during my golf tournament so I can't be there and give her away.

□ □

But why should Dick's wife throw a tantrum just because he wears golfing shoes at her mother's funeral?

□ □

In the club house, I heard Ralph's new fiancée say, "Imagine grown men becoming excited about pelting a little white ball around a big field with long sticks and getting all frantic when they can't get it to stay in a hole in the ground." O God, she really is a stupid woman.

I realize perfectly well that I did the 400-yard third hole in one, but You may not have noticed that I drove off from the sixteenth tee.

□ □

Okay, Lord, hitting my ball so it lands in the crow's nest in that tall tree is a shot in a million, but couldn't You save the miracles for converting the heathen?

It was when that priest said, “Golf isn’t everything, you know,” that I realized, Lord, that further discussion with him was absolutely pointless.

Kind and thoughtful to the end, Jeff Driver arranged to be buried on the course, Lord, so all his friends could be there.

You're quite wrong, Lord, golf is not my religion; it's far more precious to me than that.

□ □

I would have won that Christmas morning if only the binding on my skis hadn't broken.

□ □

I've never lost my temper on the golf course. It always disappears during my first practice swing.

How did I manage to miss a two-inch putt? You're supposed to know everything. *You* tell *me.*

□ □

Today, God, there were typhoons in Bangladesh, three landslides in Austria and a full-scale earthquake in Chile–and when my ball halts on the lip of the hole You can't even manage a teeny weeny tremor.

8

MY WAILY PRAYERS

Yes, Lord, I am reconciled to the inevitable, but couldn't You do something about it?

Of course Your way is best, God, but it doesn't work.

□ □

Now that my soul's dark night is lifting and the long, long agony is nearly over, may I ask You one simple question: "Where've You been?"

□ □

To be frank, Lord, I feel that You are far too concerned about my salvation and not nearly enough about my welfare.

God Almighty, don't look too long on all the miseries in Your world. We can't have You becoming an atheist.

Lord, sometimes I feel like a little sheep looking for a lost Shepherd.

Thanks for telling me You love me because that'll encourage me to go on looking for the evidence.

□ □

I know that with You all things are possible, but couldn't You tell me one thing that is certain?

□ □

I love You, God, in spite of the fact that You love me.

If You don't stop pestering me, I'm taking up transcendental meditation.

I pay You protection, God, and *still* I get my windows smashed?

Lord, the moment Mummy and Daddy told me about You forty years ago, I knew I was in for trouble sooner or later.

□ □

Dear God, don't strengthen me, I prefer to break easily.

9

I BEG YOUR PARDON

Lord, would You be so kind
as to overhaul my will
because I suspect it's not as free
as other people's.

O my God, I am heartily sorry for all the sins of my past life, and I'm sorrier still I don't feel the same way about those I'm committing now.

□ □

Dear God, please don't ask me to be better than is good for me.

□ □

If my conscience isn't bothering me, why let it bother You?

God, I can’t remember when I was first led into temptation, but I think I may have been born in it.

Lord, I *admit* I'm a hypocrite, so I can't be *all* bad.

I started to explore my motives, but after a few hours I got hopelessly lost in the maze.

□ □

You know, God, You said I've got no pride. Well, did You mean that as an insult or a compliment?

□ □

Not even You can deny that at least my failures are perfect.

If You took the trouble to get out Your binoculars,
You'd see that I *am* following.

Certainly I gave in, Lord, but
only after resisting without
a struggle.

Think Yourself into my position, Lord, and then ask Yourself if You would do anything different.

□ □

Surely You've noticed how much more relaxed I am since I lost my innocence.

□ □

Lord, having thought about the fiery punishments awaiting the wicked after death I've completely lost my will to die.

10

THE SIX-DAY WONDER

You were doing a grand job, Jehovah, so what made You give up after only six days?

□ □

When I look, O my Creator, at those billions and billions of distant stars, all quivering with radiant heat and light, I sink down upon my knees, quite overwhelmed at all that waste.

□ □

Why should I be worried about the mess the world's in, God. You're the Landlord.

I'm impressed that You created me out of nothing, but it's beginning to show.

□ □

I know You gave me freedom, but You didn't give me any choice.

But, Lord, if Man really did evolve from the apes, how did he deteriorate to this extent?

How could You do this to me? I was but an innocent newborn babe when You sold me a secondhand world.

□ □

Don't think, God, because You're invisible that I can't see through You.

□ □

Lord, when next I comment on the state of my life and say, "I didn't deserve this," it's important that You pay very close attention to my intonation.

Lord God, if only You had consulted *us* before You made the world.

Did You really have to manufacture cheap human beings with built-in obsolescence?

□ □

From the religious point of view, Lord, the trouble is that the reasons for proving You exist and don't exist are equally convincing.

□ □

All I can say is You must have done *something* to deserve me.

□ □

Every time I read through the Bible, God, I get the impression that You mellowed an awful lot as You got older.

11

SINTILLATING ME

Lord, do be a dear and try to understand. It was a straight choice between death and dishonour, and I reckoned I stood a better chance of recovering from dishonour.

To be honest, I didn't fall into sin, I jumped.

□ □

Unfortunately for me, Lord, whenever my life reaches a turning point, it always turns 360 degrees.

□ □

You remember You said You wouldn't break the bruisèd reed? Well, look at me all blackèd and bluèd.

Last night, Lord, I dreamed I made a world and put *You* in it.

I do love You, Lord, with all my heart, but can I help it if parts of me won't cooperate?

God, just think of me as a tightrope walker who had a bad bit of luck.

□ □

I have repented, but that doesn't necessarily mean I'm sorry.

□ □

The Bible definitely says You are the friend of sinners, Lord, so what could I possibly have done to fall out of favour?

I know that in Your infinite power You can read my thoughts, but tonight may I strongly recommend to You, in Your infinite wisdom, not to.

□ □

I'll only talk to You, God, on condition that anything I say will not be taken down and used in evidence against me.

□ □

One thing should be chalked up in my favour–I've never been scared to be a coward.

□ □

I'm not any better than I was but neither am I any worse, so wouldn't You say I'm making some progress?

Lord, You are the first one who ever accused me of being a *miserable* sinner.

Lord, forgive me all my sins so I can begin all over again.

□ □

I'm some kind of conservationist, Lord. My life has been one long waste continually recycled.

□ □

Believe me, I'm *not* boasting, I'm confessing.

□ □

Just look on me as a human being writ small.

12

SWALLOWING THE TABLETS OF THE LAW

Dear Sweet Lord, didn't You hear me say I've given *You* up for Lent?

All right, Jehovah, so I broke the Ten Commandments, but didn't Moses?

□ □

When I was at school, Lord, nine out of ten was considered a very good mark.

□ □

If You love me, *keep* Your commandments.

Thank You, God. If You hadn't provided me with a complete list of the commandments, I'd never have discovered all those interesting sins on my own.

For a whole year and a half,
Lord, I've not been guilty of
a single sensuous thought.
Not once have I felt the
stirrings of the flesh or lusted
after my neighbour's wife.
So what I want to
know is, what have I done to
deserve this?

You know You said to St. Paul, "My grace is sufficient for thee." Well, we've got news for You.

I do assure You, that lies disgust me, too, and I look forward to the time when they won't be necessary.

□ □

Sure, Lord, in theory truth is beauty and beauty is truth, but how do You account for the fact that whenever I tell my family the truth it leads to very ugly scenes?

Lord, I never mean to break the commandments but sometimes when I'm experimenting with how far they'll stretch they suddenly snap.

□ □

Would You mind repeating that bit about "the eternal flame and the worm that dieth not"–I need all the discouragement I can get.

No, we don't have to choose between You and Mammon—we've already chosen.

I'm a father myself, so what I want to know is, "If You really didn't want Your children to sin, why did You forbid it?"

□ □

I realize it's a terrible sin to murder my boss, but I can't think of a less violent solution to my problems.

□ □

Don't give me the gift of endurance, Lord. I couldn't bear it.

13

GOOD NEWS IS NO NEWS

If this is the Good News,
Lord, spare me the bad.

The reason I've got this terrible hangover today is because yesterday I took Your advice and gave no thought for the morrow.

□ □

Now that You have filled me to the brim with Christian joy, could You spare me a bit of happiness to go with it?

□ □

I would have offered that beefy guy the other cheek, Lord, but when I recovered consciousness, he'd gone.

God, I never gamble on principle, but strictly because I like it.

I never hate those who hate me, Lord. I'm just grateful that I'm not loved by such hateful people.

But I had to break my fast, Lord—I was hungry.

You know, You said misfortune and adversity are good for me. Well, are You sure that English is Your mother tongue?

Can You explain to me, God, why so many of Your best friends and admirers are out-and-out nuts?

Be fair, Lord, remember You chose me, I didn't choose You.

□ □

There's one drawback to Your recipe for a happy life: it doesn't seem to have any ingredients.

□ □

Dear God, if You're thinking of providing for me today as You did yesterday, forget it.

□ □

Having looked into the future, I am now smoking heavily to reduce my life expectancy.

14

MY GOD AND I

You're omniscient, God, and I'm stupid;
You're omnipotent and I'm weak;
You're eternal and I'm but a creature of a day.
Why don't You pick on someone Your own size?

Neither You nor I can possibly be satisfied with the way the world is. Your will isn't done on earth and mine certainly isn't. So, Lord, if You pray for me, I promise to pray for You.

God, I've always tried to treat You in a Christian way
and look how You treat me.

I often think back to the first time I flew to Los Angeles. How I kept admiring the achievements of the human race. On the runway I marvelled at the power in those jets. The plane itself was beautiful to the eyes and an engineering miracle. And as it soared noiselessly into the blue, I looked down on the great city carpeted below with its high-rise apartments, its factories, its monuments, and felt proud to be a man. Next stop Mars, then Venus, then . . . Ah, but there is no end to man's incredible potential. I confess I wasn't thinking of You at all until at 30,000 feet the plane developed engine trouble and, in a flash, I felt I loved You, Father, and was somehow nearer to You than I had ever been.

So I don't have to come back straight away, why did You make dinosaurs in the first place?

Lord, I can't help admiring You for the way You manage to keep on smiling through my tears.

□ □

It's not fair to attack me, God. I'm a pacifist.

□ □

For a considerable time I've been dissatisfied with the measure of the divine response to my petitions. This is why, after much soul-searching, I beseech You, Allah, help me.

□ □

Could it be, God, that our only mistake was that we expected too much of each other?

But, Lord, couldn't You have told me that at the end of the tunnel was another tunnel?

□ □

If I loved You as much as You love me, wouldn't You tell *me* to lay off?

□ □

Could it be that You are too proud to admit that You dislike me just a little?

□ □

But, Lord, how would You be able to exercise Your finest attributes of mercy and loving-kindness if there weren't people like me around?

15

WHEN MY NUMBER IS UP

What d'You mean, my Papal Indulgence isn't worth the parchment it's written on?

As I said to that atheist, Lord, "If there's no hell, how are you going to get *your* reward?"

I would gladly have given my life to You, O God, but it was the only one I had.

□ □

What irony if after all this You send me a happy death.

□ □

I know that one day You will send me the bill, but please don't expect a tip.

□ □

When I look back on the dreadful sins of my youth, Lord, and try to repent of them, I always end up feeling envious.

Can't we take a bit of the heat out of our discussion on the afterlife?

□ □

Almighty God, if You think You can scare me with all that medieval stuff about hellfire, You're absolutely right.

□ □

I know I was drunk, Lord, but why threaten me with eternal fire for it when the police only put me in the cooler for the night?

Judging from sermons, God, there's not all *that* difference between heaven and hell.

I don't mind dying in my sleep, but make sure You warn me just before I drop off.

□ □

Lord, can't You at least tell me the *year* I'm going to die in, so I can budget ahead?

□ □

Naturally I believe in ghosts. My first wife still haunts me, and she's not even dead yet.

□ □

For as long as I'm unrepentant, Lord, never say die.

If You're not nice to me, God, I'll commit suicide and You won't get another chance.

□ □

I'm very keen on Your brochure of Paradise but I don't think I can face the journey.

□ □

At the present rate of inflation, Lord, a heavenly hundred-fold won't be nearly enough.

□ □

I know that You will raise me up on the Last Day, but at this moment I'd settle for a bit of first aid.

□ □

When night falls, Father, and the shadow of my days grows long, and when my eyes are dimmed and my breath begins to fail and the time of eternal reckoning draws near, would it not be fairer, Father, if You and I went down on our knees and recited our act of contrition together?